THE GREAT SILVER MANUFACTORY

THE GREAT
SILVER MANUFACTORY

Matthew Boulton
and the Birmingham silversmiths
1760~1790

Eric Delieb

Research Collaboration by
Michael Roberts

STUDIO VISTA

Produced by November Books Limited, 23–29 Emerald Street, London WC1N 3QL.

Published by Studio Vista Publishers, Blue Star House, Highgate Hill, London N19.

Typeset in Baskerville by Yendall & Company Limited, Riscatype House, 22–25 Red Lion Court, Fleet Street, London EC4.

Printed by Compton Printing Limited, Pembroke Road, Stocklake, Aylesbury, Bucks.

Bound by Leighton-Straker Binders, Standard Road, London NW10.

© November Books Limited 1971.

Printed in Great Britain.

This edition is not for sale in the United States of America or Canada.

Designed by Thomas Carter.
Copy preparation: John Leath.

SBN *289 70204 6*

Dedicated to

MY FATHER AND HIS DEAR WIFE, CELIA

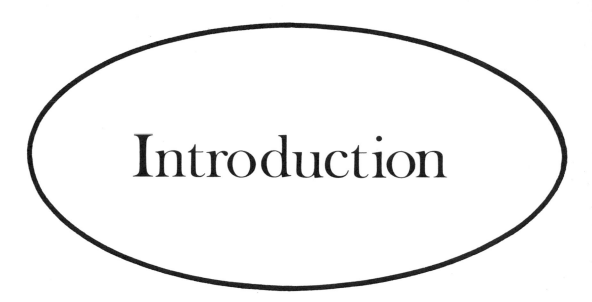

Introduction

England at the middle of the 18th century was in the midst of the transition from a rural economy and way of life to an urban one, brought about by the Agrarian and Industrial Revolutions. Despite the catastrophic bursting of the South Sea Bubble in 1720 and the economically debilitating costs of wars with France and Spain, scientific, agricultural and mercantile progress was vital enough to affect an enormous amount of the population, if in varying degrees. George II was on the throne, and the affairs of government were managed by a select group of nobles, or rich powerful families. It was a period of Whig control, and while Walpole may have done nothing basically for the peasants or the poor, he did encourage economic prosperity by reducing import and export duties, and by striving to preserve the peace brought about by the Treaty of Utrecht in 1714. The American colonies were soon to rebel against the taxes imposed by the mother country in order to recoup some of the cost of her wars with France and Spain, and to claim their own independence.

Success in trade brought about a wider distribution of money which swelled the ranks of the middle class: prosperous farmers, merchants who had taken advantage of fashion to introduce new styles, and of course, manufacturers and entrepreneurs. These people had money, although not as much as the landed gentry, but were determined to create their own life style, in which they could share in the material pleasures and even luxuries previously available to only a very few. They wanted impressive homes, fashionable clothes, and household items which would serve as obvious signs of their success and new-found standing.

The arrival of this new class created myriad requirements in clothing, for instance, items such as buckles, buttons, and other fashionable accessories. While metropolitan silversmiths were quite content to produce massive plate for the rich, the Midland manufactories began to make richly embellished buttons, some of which are illustrated on page 40; steel chains for both men and women, dangling with fobs and seals; gilt-metal 'toys' or small pieces of jewellery, such as pinchbeck rings, or brooches, watch-keys, and tapestry hooks, or little hooks for hanging jewels on bodices.

The costumes of the period gave the gentlemen wide-skirted greatcoats with many buttons and gorgeously embroidered waistcoats or undercoats. They wore buttoned-up breeches, and solid-looking buckled shoes. Ladies wore full-bodied gowns, embroidered with tassels and frogging, and with tightly enlaced bodices. Their bonnets were shallow and be-ribboned, or they might have instead elaborately coiffeured curls with mantilla-shaped fans stuck into the hair. Shoes were high heeled and enriched with multi-coloured fabrics. The younger ladies wore capes or shawls, and some wore wide-brimmed hats upon scarves: all forms of costumes were embellished with clever and beautiful small jewellery pieces.

Provincial gentlemen, attempting to emulate their London counterparts, demanded elaborately enriched snuff-boxes, and contemporary prints of middle-class men taking snuff are quite amusing. Also, while they wanted spectacular buttons, they wanted to pay less than for London-produced silver goods. The Midland ones, though cheaper, were none the less often breathtakingly beautiful. Sets of them were sold for pennies, and even the dearer examples manufactured in steel, presumed to be longer lasting than brass or pinchbeck, were within the range of the new customers.

The demand for vast quantities of such items could not be satisfied by individual craftsmen operating on their own, and a few far-sighted men, realising this, established themselves as entrepreneurs, controlling, in their manufactories, numerous skilled men and often hundreds of workers, filling orders and creating items for the new rich in a much more efficient and profitable manner. The production of silver articles offers a prime example of this development, for silver, and eventually also silver plate, was especially required by the middle class as another outward sign of their prosperity.

The history of silver produced in England harks back to the medieval monasteries, where a dedicated man might work for forty years upon one masterpiece and devote all of his imagination, skill and craftsmanship to making an elaborate item for use in the Church. This was his offering to God, and it seems certain that many of the finest extant works of art stemmed from the Church and its monks. Even the shapes of domestic articles are echoes of ecclesiastical objects: a bulbous flagon gradually diminished into a utilitarian coffee pot; while the communion set, with its cups, patens and spoons, gave way to domestic wine-cups, salvers and serving spoons.

Many thousands of silversmiths' names are recorded, over the whole of England and part of Ireland, yet few of these were men of imagination. As far as can be ascertained, each silversmith had his own workshop, manned by specialists of all sorts: 'raisers', namely, men who beat a piece of flat silver into a hollow vessel; 'burnishers', who polished the article after it had been produced; and 'planishers', who further polished the surfaces with special smoothing hammers. Each silversmith also employed a few apprentices who eventually graduated to become 'journeymen', or men who had served their apprenticeship and were able to work for their masters on their own account.

There was little cottage-trade, but there were outworkers, and many of the smaller silversmiths all over England handed over their small items to be finished by these people. This is certainly true of Birmingham-produced silver of the late 18th and early 19th centuries, where one man might produce a box, give it to another to embellish and then, in turn, pass it to a third for gilding. If the item was, for instance, a vinaigrette, the grille would be placed inside by another specialist. Hinge-making was also farmed out, so that while an article bore the maker's mark of one factory, it is probable that it was the product of many different hands.

Current taste was dominated by foreign influences, such as the Huguenot-French style or the plainer German forms. The rococo style, which will be more fully discussed later, was also prevalent. This enrichment consisted of lavish scrolling ornament. Each such article was flooded with a mass of embellishment, until the lines which the earlier English silver had attained were completely lost. However, when these French-inspired articles first arrived on the scene they were seized upon by an avid public; but as is the nature of things, rococo ornament became stale and, by the 1760s, a new style was much needed.

Whatever the style, the quality of English silver was, as always, very good, chiefly through the influence of the Assay Offices, which insisted that a high content of precious metal should be used in all production. The leading cities, such as London, Chester, Exeter, Newcastle and York, in England; Edinburgh, and Glasgow in Scotland; and Dublin, Cork and such smaller places as Limerick, Youghal, Galway and Kilkenny in Ireland, all had Assay Offices. Woe betide a silversmith who presented an article which fell below the required 925 parts of silver per thousand of alloy; the article was smashed, and the craftsman warned.

There is a famous incident which illustrates the dangers of attempting to deceive the Assay Offices. Paul de Lamerie, the great Huguenot silversmith, worked in massive cast silverware. Eventually, as happens with the most honest workmen, he became rather blasé about the success of his craftsmanship. When commissioned to produce a magnificent ewer and basin for the Lord Chancellor, he baulked at paying the enormous 'ounceage' which would be entailed, even if it was only pence per ounce. Surprisingly, for a man of such integrity, he sent a salt-cellar to be hall-marked at the London Assay Office and when it was returned, he cut around the base where the marks were placed and inserted this disc into the base of the massive ewer. It was only by chance, some two centuries later, that the fraud was discovered. The Plate Committee, which sits at the London Assay Office to safeguard all items placed before it as doubtful, ordered the base of the ewer to be heated; the circlet of silver, with the inserted hall-marks, dropped out!

Such were the demands and standards in silver production when Matthew Boulton took over his father's manufactory in 1759. He was one of the first people to realise the implications of serving the middle class with mass-produced items, although he eventually served the King, the nobility and the aristocracy as well. Beginning in a small way as a buckle-maker, he grew into a powerful entrepreneur. His success was brought about by his imagination and unquenchable optimism, which overcame his years of financial worry and family tragedy.

Matthew Boulton

Birmingham, to judge from the many early histories and topographies which survive, was a flourishing city from A.D. 750. West (quoting Dugdale) and Hutton, both historians on Birmingham, gave a full topography of that city, its size and its elements, remarking in particular, that the citizens of Birmingham were noted for their longevity which in the 18th and early 19th centuries was rare; indeed, one man lived to the hale age of 107.

Statistics from Hutton's *History* show that from the Restoration until 1731 there had been a marked increase in the number of inhabitants. Hutton's work also stated that 'the tool, coarse iron ware, lacquered articles', and, by implication, the 'toys' (small silverware, steel chains, bracelets, personal jewellery, swords and sword hilts, buttons, buckles, etc., made in silver and other semi- and non-precious metals and materials) 'all emanated from the High Street area.'

Matthew Boulton, senior, came to Birmingham from Lichfield in search of wider opportunities, following the example of his uncle, Zachary Babington, and was apprenticed, probably before 1710, to a stamper and 'toymaker'. Among other early followers of the craft were Robert Moore, Oliver Round, John Taylor, Joseph Carpenter, William Price and Christopher Sole. Before 1723, the name of Matthew Boulton was added to the list of master-men, for in the marriage register of St Martin's Church is the following entry: '1723, June 21, Matthew Boulton to Christiana Peers.' He could not easily have married before he became a master, and this entailed serving as an apprentice and then as a journeyman. Under these conditions, he would not have been able to marry before 1723.

Upon his marriage he settled in a small house in Whitehall Lane or Steelhouse Lane – the exact position of which cannot now be identified. In 1731, 7 Snow Hill became empty and was then taken by Matthew, senior. Thereafter, his name appears regularly in the rate-books as the occupant, until his death in 1759.

By the time that Matthew Boulton, the son, was born in 1728, his father had become a reasonably wealthy button and buckle manufacturer. Young Boulton received a private education from the Reverend John Hausted, although his father was wealthy enough to send him to the local grammar school, and on his father's death, the business passed to Matthew. There was an elder brother, John, who could have taken command of the family business, for the other elder brothers died young, but Matthew showed obvious business ability.

It is known that Matthew was not content to wait until his father's death, and had commenced trading on his own, when aged about 30. He purchased steel from the Sheffield inventor of cast steel, Benjamin Huntsman, began to produce buckles, and probably employed skilled men to work for him, for there is no evidence that Boulton ever made anything with his own hands.

Boulton's obvious dislike for London has often been pondered upon, as have the reasons for his tremendous endeavours to obtain the establishment of an Assay Office at Birmingham, refusing in the meantime to send his silverware to be hall-marked at London – he preferred to send it to Chester. The time taken in getting the articles to Chester and returned to Birmingham after marking must have been far greater than if they had been dispatched to London. Roads were bad everywhere, but it might be supposed that transport would have been faster on the road to the capital.

The conclusion is possibly that Boulton was rather like the well-known English country squire who was a big fish in a small pond – the magistrate, benefactor and squire in his own little hamlet – but when he finally took the great step of visiting London, was made fun of by the fops of the town, had his hat pulled down over his ears and was finally and ignominiously robbed of his purse, leaving him only too glad to scuttle back to his own country domain.

Boulton, as a young Warwickshire stalwart, might have met with the same fate. He had come to London to sell prints for John Boydell, the famous printer, print-seller and eventual Lord Mayor, and was eager to make his fortune. He was not of particularly large stature and probably had a broad country brogue, which would not have been to the liking of the dandies of the streets. Many other men experienced the same mortification, in this age of increasing social mobility. Boulton may have decided to avoid journeys to the capital until he could face all comers with complete equanimity. When, in the late 1760s, Boulton again visited London, he came as the possessor of a large manufactory, and his position was then quite different: within ten years he had established himself, mixed freely with nobility, and had been received at Court. Boulton's speech was now carefully phrased and he had a cosmopolitan savoir faire.

Boulton had a tragic private life. His first wife was Mary Robinson of Lichfield (born in 1727), whom he married in 1749 and who died in 1759. They had children, but these either died young or were still-born. He then married his deceased wife's

Register entry for Matthew Boulton's marriage to Anne Robinson.

introduced Wedgwood to the Lunar Society, as canals were important to many of its members; Boulton had an interest in them, since they could be used to convey his products cheaply. Erasmus Darwin was a great raconteur, and even Dr Samuel Johnson could not talk him down. It is evident that these two giants could not, or would not, tolerate each other, as both liked to dominate their circle.

Another influential member of the society was Dr Joseph Priestly, a chemist, an experimenter in such fields as the nature of electricity and its application to gilding, air for combustion engines, balloons, mesmerism and gases, and an active anti-slavery agitator. In May 1780, he retired and came to Birmingham. His years in that city were amongst the happiest in his life. He was patronised by Lord Shelburne and acted as his librarian. Unfortunately, the notorious Birmingham Riots of 1791, in which the homes of so-named dissenters were destroyed, affected him badly; his home, library and laboratory were destroyed. He fled to London and settled in Hackney, where he re-established his laboratory. The Lunars sent him both money and materials for his experiments and apparatus. He appealed for damages, but was unsuccessful, and thereupon left England in 1794 for Pennsylvania, where he built another laboratory, established a printing press and was actively engaged in scientific work until his death. He expressed his feelings for his fellow members of the Lunar Society in a memoir, naming all the important figures who had influenced him.

Sir Joseph Banks, although not an official member of the society, was active in it. As Mr Banks, he had sailed to Australia in 1768 with the ill-fated Captain James Cook and had taken with him green glass earrings, which had been manufactured at Soho by Boulton's toy-man, Thacker. These were for distribution to the natives of the far-off and possibly hostile country. Cook also ordered what must have been a navigational instrument from Boulton in 1776, and his letter of acknowledgement informed him that the making of the object might take years. This must have been a troublesome piece to make, for Boulton was always excusing himself from making articles which might take several months or extra effort to produce. Captain Cook sailed on 25 June 1776, never to return, and there was no further mention of the nature of the article.

Later, on a second journey, Cook sailed to New South Wales, taking with him marking-rings, which Banks and Boulton had designed, to tag a strain of Merino sheep which he proposed to introduce there. These tags were double-ring-shaped, and when clasped together, could mark the sheep so that a tally could be maintained on the number.

Finally, one should mention the master printer, John Baskerville. An early member of the Society, he was a non-conformist, non-believer, and free-thinker all his life, which resulted in a terrible abuse of his corpse after his death in 1775. The churchmen were reluctant to place him in consecrated ground and he was eventually buried in a plot of ground under which ran one of Birmingham's canals. The land was purchased some twenty years later by a businessman, who exposed the embalmed body of Baskerville to the public, for a small charge, until a gentleman obtained permission from the rector of St Philip's Church to have the body placed in a vault, the property of a churchwarden named George Barker.

Motteux, one of Boulton's agents, had tried for years without success to sell Baskerville's type-faces for his widow. With the printing presses, they were eventually sold after much trouble to a French society which wished to reprint the works of Voltaire – a fitting end to their history, although there was a rumour that some of Baskerville's original types were to be found in England in the 1820s.

Even in a group such as the Lunar Society, composed of people of diverse and admirable abilities, Boulton was one of the leaders, or perhaps the leading light, as his talents were so wide ranging and numerous. A list of the members and associates of the Lunar Society is given in Appendix I.

Above
Print of the Soho Manufactory, dated 1781.

Left
Etching accompanying the rules of conduct of the Soho Insurance Company. 'A member of this society with his arm in a sling, is seated on a cube, which is an emblem of stability, as the dog at his feet is of fidelity; he is attended by Art, Prudence and Industry, the latter of whom raiseth him with one hand, and with the other sheweth him Plenty, expressed by the cornucopia lying at the feet of Commerce, from whence it flows. Art resteth on a table of the mechanic powers, and looks up to Minerva, goddess of arts and wisdom, who, descending in the clouds, directs to the Soho Manufactory, near which are little boys busy in designing, etc. which shew that an early application to the study of arts is an effectual means to improve them; the flowers that are strewed over the bee-hive represent the sweets that Industry is ever crowned with.'

The Manufactory

Matthew Boulton inherited his father's business, on the latter's death, in 1759. It then employed only a handful of men and specialised in the production of buckles, buttons and other small items for which Birmingham was known. Young Boulton's enterprises began to show themselves in the letter-books from 1757 with details of the smaller items which, in spite of the plethora of magnificent silver-wrought plate which the partnership of Boulton and Fothergill later produced, always comprised the backbone of their joint endeavours.

Boulton had quickly outgrown his father's old premises at Snow Hill and found a large plot of land for expansion on Handsworth Heath beside the road to Wolverhampton. The site was not in Warwickshire, as was Birmingham, but just over the border in Staffordshire. What attracted him to this site was the Hockley Brook, a tributary of the Tame, which would supply the water-driven power for his lathes. (When Hockley Brook dried up, Boulton eagerly sought James Watt senior's assistance for steam-driven engines.) It was here that the famous Soho Manufactory was erected between 1759 and 1766, by direction of Samuel Wyatt, brother of both William Wyatt and the famous James Wyatt, PRA. The original estimate for Soho House was £2,000, but the final cost was in the region of £10,000.

There are several prints of the building. In one, the brook is clearly seen on the far right, while the silver manufactory was at the back of the building, where there may have been a water-mill. The large rectangular edifice with many windows served as a warehouse and provided the heads of department with their offices. There would have been various rooms holding stock (saleable and otherwise), materials for future work, lapidaries-shops, mounting-shops, and the other branches of an enormous manufactory. This print, dated 1781, bears a caption in French, for it was intended to advertise the manufactory in France. Boulton wanted to show his French clients and competitors that he had a busy manufactory, and Soho is cleverly depicted, teeming with activity. There are arrivals in coaches, men on horseback, two figures in the forecourt who seem to be appraising the building, and another coach-and-four leaving.

A print of the manufactory engraved for Shaw's *Staffordshire* was made by Francis Eginton in 1798. The buildings are the same, but the out-buildings at the back can be more clearly discerned. It is as if another building had been erected, and the various chimneys showed that the use of furnaces was an essential part of the work. Of course, all metalwork depends on the application of heat to braze (to solder with various alloys), to melt the metals, and to cast the ornaments and embellishments. Certainly

BACK-ELEVATION.

LONGITUDINAL SECTION TH^E FRONT

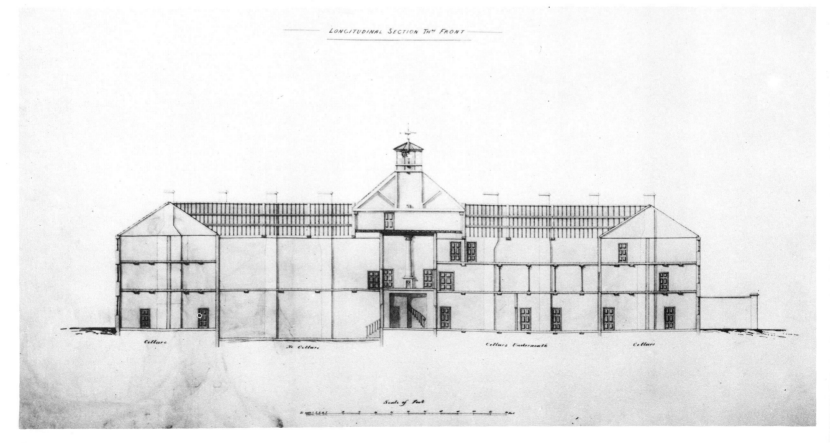

Cellars   No Cellars   Cellars Underneath   Cellars

Scale of Feet

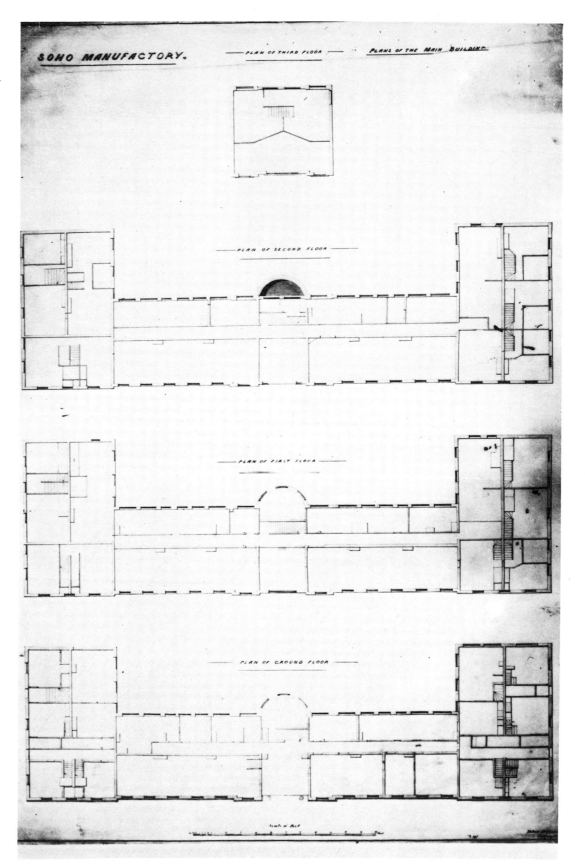

SOHO MANUFACTORY.

PLAN OF THIRD FLOOR — PLANS OF THE MAIN BUILDING

PLAN OF SECOND FLOOR

PLAN OF FIRST FLOOR

PLAN OF GROUND FLOOR

letter of complaint with complete sang-froid, talked blithely about future sales and orders, and made no reference to money at all!

Financial difficulties began to make themselves very noticeable in 1772, and there were other troubles. Fothergill wrote to Boulton in May: 'The mill pool is very low. I spoke last night to Kimnell [one of Boulton's most senior workers] to order ye mill to go only six hours ye day – as we have but very few orders for steel goods – Dr Small wishes you could pick up a proper hand in London, the person in John Harrison's shop does not seem much at work in going with anything material.'

The desperate condition regarding funds continued. In 1773, Fothergill wrote to Boulton: 'I am sorry to observe the distressed situation of things and will direct Mr Scale make further reduction in our hands at Soho.' On 6 January, Fothergill again wrote: 'Even *we* have not been able to procure the weekly £21 for Mr Z. Walker in the whole town, for since the supply at Soho has been on £200, they have not been able to space the usual weekly sum for this place. We fall indeed, considerably short in our remittances to Mr Matthews and can only hope that you have been able to procure for him some of our debts in London. Mr Matthews had drawn £150 in favour of Mr Stonier, which must be paid out of the money we appeal from Darby on Monday evening.' The tale of woe goes on. Fothergill wrote to his partner on 17 February: 'The shortage of cash continues here so great that it is absolutely impossible to procure any boxwood that will be of service. Please to order 500 oz finest silver as it is greatly needed.'

This last remark in Fothergill's letter is surprising: if funds were so low that they could not adequately pay outstanding wages and were obliged to lay off hands, how could they commit themselves to a purchase of 500 ounces of silver? But, of course, that was part of Boulton's business expertise – one day he was virtually insolvent; the next, he was a rich man and the whole town fawned before him. If all his friends about town had known about the impoverished state of Soho, they might not have been so forthcoming with loans, as Fothergill's letters reveal.

Bad coins were being passed, and Fothergill wrote to Boulton again on the same day: 'Pray do not neglect sending Mr Z. Walker a pair of scales proper for weighing money, as it is highly wanted, having many bad pieces by us.'

In 1773, the situation was still despondent. In March, Fothergill told Boulton: 'I also see by Scale's accounts to you that he only paid away £150 to the workmen last Saturday, I will enquire of him tomorrow what he did with the remaining £50, as he sent none to Mr Matthews, neither did he furnish any to "ZW"' [Zacheus Walker]. There seemed to be no end to Fothergill's gloom. Again, in March 1773, he wrote to Boulton (who had also written him a melancholy letter): 'We have procured this day on £20 from Chawner [probably a London silversmith] which will send on Wednesday perhaps with some more', and eventually, 'Chawner had a draft yesterday for £100 and has this day sent 70 guineas in part, but a number of them are so small that we dare not send them to Mr Matthews, yet he says that they take them here without scruple at the exise office.'

On 15 March 1773, Fothergill sent Boulton a full account of outstanding amounts, including foreign debts, which in April/May 1773 amounted to £7492. 2s. 6d. It appears that this sum was an enormous amount for one month's debt, and it is therefore no wonder that Fothergill, who was really a junior partner, was so worried about finances. On 24 April, there was a brief note of accounts: owing, £10,000; stocks, £5,000.

Still complaining, Fothergill wrote to Boulton on 13 May 1773: '. . . we are entirely out of luck respecting money matters as we have this day ransacked the whole town for cash without effect and our situation becomes every day more critical and serious, for God's sake, do try to procure some money before you leave London either by

A very rare pair of rococo candlesticks: the bases formed of floral swirls and of incurving octagonal shapes, the columns enriched with acanthus, beading and fruit ornament. These candlesticks could have been made by any London silversmith, and Boulton and Fothergill's adoption of the style is very puzzling. It is possible that these articles, which are loaded with pitch, were commissioned by a Londoner whom Boulton and Fothergill could not refuse, and, since they would not send articles to London for marking, these were marked at Chester (see *right*).
Maker: Boulton and Fothergill, 1768.
Size: height 12 in, diameter at base 6 in.
Weights: 1) 33.33 oz.
         2) 33.25 oz.
It is difficult to identify the designer of these candlesticks, but they may have been copied from a London-made pair.

articles. Consider the 'Neptune' button or the delightfully-enriched, cut-steel sword, inlaid with jasperware plaques and wonder at how two materials – pottery and metal – could marry so well, the one setting off the beauty of the other. It would be difficult to differentiate between their qualities, since each complements the other.

The production of silverware was almost accidental, for Boulton was more interested in producing fine fashionable small items for the new wealthy consumer. He applied himself with all his energies to seeking out good workmen. Some of these craftsmen he paid well, but treated others very badly. This was an inexplicable trait in Boulton, but he was subject to the same pressures as any manufacturer on a great scale, and he ought to be forgiven for a few misdemeanours during a long and worthwhile life. The result of his energies was that when the Adam-inspired neo-classical period began, Boulton and Fothergill were to lead the way.

Their foresight and energy created new difficulties: in addition to the ever-present shortage of cash, other craftsmen, who were themselves plagiarised, retaliated and copied Boulton's most beautiful pieces. His styles were derivative at first, but they were in turn universally copied when neo-classicism emerged.

A piece of Boulton and Fothergill silver is very rarely inelegant. It may possess massive gauge, which was not accidental, for someone who was not accustomed to buying fine pieces would be more amenable if he felt that he was getting good value for his money. Chapter Five, on ornament, will show with what care Boulton and Fothergill selected their designers. It was only after Boulton's death, with the establishment of the Boulton Plate Company, that one finds somewhat tasteless objects, which mirrored the styles of that time.

It might be advantageous to compare the Soho silverware with the styles which preceded it. The foreign-inspired fashions of Elizabethan silver were followed by the Puritan demands for plainness and clarity of line. In turn came the exuberance of the Restoration, which in reaction to a period of restraint produced objects of ornate decoration. With the advent of the Huguenots came another wave of French influence, introducing massive enrichment, heavy casting and matt-chasing as typical styling. The Hanoverian period was much calmer: lines became more symmetrical, plain surfaces were much admired and the use of high-standard Britannia silver gave the metal its beautiful sheen. It has been rightly claimed that a piece of George I or Queen Anne silver could 'smite a man down', for it was wrought of such heavy gauge metal.

Above
Charles 1 clean-lined communion cup. It is a replacement of an earlier cup presented to an Exeter bishop by Queen Elizabeth I.

Left
The exuberant, silver gilt, large, Charles II, porringer and cover, dated 1677, and the late rococo, lavishly enriched candlesticks, dated 1763, are typical of Restoration silver.

The arrival of rococo designs with extravagance of ornament delighted some people, but appalled others. When, therefore, Boulton and Fothergill presented an eager public with different ideas, success was not too far away, but far enough for poor Fothergill, who would not realise that silverware might lead Boulton to fame and praise. Fortunately for posterity, Boulton took little notice of him.

44

The Silver

By 1771, the Soho Manufactory was beginning to launch into its great production period. For his superb silverware, *bijouterie* and *objets d'art*, Boulton was no longer dependent on other people's designs, which he had stolen, but could employ men of talent to design for him. As well as Robert Adam, John Flaxman and James Wyatt, he used a Soho workman named Hooker, about whom nothing else is known, to act as draughtsman, and it was probably this man's sketches which were submitted to clients for their approval. Sheets of sketches were sent round from person to person, and the customer indicated which article took his fancy. Frequently, a would-be purchaser might not immediately return these sketches, and frantic but still courteously phrased letters were dispatched requesting their return.

There had been few large pieces of silverware produced in Birmingham for centuries, and thus there was no Assay Office. Boulton made tremendous endeavours to obtain the establishment of an Assay Office there, refusing to send his silverware to be hall-marked in London. Meanwhile, he sent his silverware to be hall-marked in Chester where James Foliott, a merchant of that city, acted as his agent. In 1771, when the first mention is made of articles being sent to Chester, Foliott was informed: 'herewith you'll receive by the Chester coach a silver cup which beg you'll get marked and returned by the same conveyance.' This was wishful thinking, for it sometimes took months for articles to be returned to Birmingham.

It is probable that the rococo candlesticks illustrated on page 42, together with a finely-pierced mazerine, dated 1769–70, are the only two pieces of Chester-marked silver emanating from Boulton and Fothergill at present identified, although in 1778 there was mention of a gold spoon for which an agent was charged £17. This spoon was not recorded at the Birmingham Assay Office, nor could it be traced through Chester's papers which, since that office closed some years ago, are in a state of disarray. Canon Ridgeway, the eminent authority on Chester silver, had never heard of this gold spoon, but it might have been produced for Wentworth House in Yorkshire, as the agent had previously supplied a pair of candlesticks to that location. Boulton was ever hopeful that the Act for the Establishment of an Assay Office in Birmingham would be passed in May 1773 and wrote a long letter to Fothergill on the 8th of that month in which he talked rather wildly about bribing ministers with fine steel sword-hilts, and stated that he had talked with Lord Denbeigh, who had talked to the King, who, in turn, had asked for a fine steel sword-hilt. Happily for Boulton, the Assay Office was established in Birmingham that year.

Boulton mentioned too a 'pair of small saddle vases, metal bodies, which were not fellows, and returned by a damn'd swearing chap, and Clayton allowed him!' Many of the objects listed above merited great attention, primarily because they were exhibition goods, made expressly to be sold to the general public and not to favoured customers, who might be permitted to visit Boulton in Birmingham. Also, many were by master-craftsmen, among them Wedgwood; the sidereal clock, for instance, was almost certainly by Whitehurst, and the ormulu would have been of the finest quality that Boulton could produce. One might imagine the turmoil at Soho while Boulton was producing these *pièces de résistance* for the London sale.

The Watkin Lewes table

In the middle of 1774, a Worcester jeweller-cum-silversmith, one Samuel Bradley, was approached by a group of Worcester ladies with a request for a silver table. (It must be emphasised here that Bradley was acting purely as a factor.) The term table was an archaic word for what is now known as a large tray, used in this case as a receptacle for tea utensils, dinner plates and the like. The recipient of this table was to be one 'Sir Gwatkin Lewis'. The poorly-educated scribe who had entered the order into the letter-book misspelt the recipient's name badly; only in *Berrow's Worcester Journal* (incidentally, the oldest English news-sheet, founded in the 1660s) was the history of what must have been a most impressive piece of silverware revealed.

Sir Watkin Lewes was of Welsh extraction and was a barrister at the Chancery Bar from 1766. He married a rich heiress, who brought him considerable estates in Glamorgan and Pembrokeshire. After unsuccessfully contesting the parliamentary seat at Worcester four times, claiming each time that the election had been rigged (as it frequently was in those days), he eventually forsook politics for civics. He was knighted in 1773, became an alderman of the City of London and was Lord Mayor in 1780, in which year he was also one of the four members of Parliament for the City of London. The later part of his life was clouded with financial difficulties, and he died within the rules of the notorious Fleet Prison.

To return to the table: there appear to be two versions of its size. The Assay Office records at Birmingham state that its total weight was 327 ounces, but Boulton, writing to Sir Harbord Harbord in 1775, stated that it weighed 334 ounces. On Boulton's reckoning, the total price he charged Bradley came to 140 guineas, including the cost of the engraving of the emblems on the surface of the top. A great deal of discussion went on between Boulton and Bradley as to the motifs which 'the ladies of Worcester' would wish to have engraved upon the table. Boulton even offered to take impressions of the inscriptions so that the subscribers might see for themselves the beauties of the engraving. *Berrow's Worcester Journal* stated, on Thursday, 18 August 1774:

> Yesterday was presented to Lady Lewes, by the ladies of Worcester, the superb piece of plate mentioned in our last, adorned with many curious and emblematic devices of which the following is an exact description:
> The shield
>   a) in the middle: Fortitude
>   b) beneath: Britannia
>   c) with Magna Carta in her hand
>   d) Temperance
> The supporters:
>   a) Eloquence
>   b) Hope
> The crest: Fame
> The motto: 'Firm in the glorious enterprize.'

Inscription: 'The ladies of Worcester present to Lady Lewes this mark of their esteem in the acknowledgement of the noble and disinterested efforts of Sir Watkin Lewes to destroy the influence of bribery and corruption in the election of members to represent their country in Parliament, and in particular to restore to the citizens of Worcester their rights and priviledges.'

A rich and elegant complete set of Worcester china, of a very curious pattern, manufactured solely for the purpose, was presented with the above piece.

Boulton wrote a much more detailed description of the table to Sir Harbord Harbord: 'This table has a solid border, bending outwards, with festoons of laurels upon it in a section of it. The bottom was an ellipsis whose length was 2 feet 7½ inches, and whose breadth was about 1 foot 11¾ inches, or perhaps 2 feet. It measured about 1½ inches wider and longer at the rim, and was 2 inches high about the flat part. In this table, a solid board was pressed on account of its strength, but if a laced border should be required, it will have more work, and become lighter, and in that case, the price will be dearer, say, from 20s. to £2 according to its degree of richness. We made no stand for this table as the "spirit of patriotism" amongst the Worcester ladies did not extend so far. We made designs for a stand of black ebony to be decorated with silver ornaments and suitable to the table but it was never executed.'

Furthermore, Boulton did not inform Harbord that if he charged Samuel Bradley 140 guineas, the latter must have priced the table at £200, if not more. It was therefore not surprising that the ardour of the ladies of Worcester cooled when the 'stand of ebony ornamented with silver' was proposed!

With Watkin Lewes's bankruptcy, the table, so richly endowed by his admirers, was probably melted down to pay some of his debts or to provide him with some sort of livelihood. Perhaps this superb article survives, but all efforts to trace it have failed.

On 8 May 1773, Matthew Boulton wrote to Fothergill, ordering him to instruct Mr Eginton and William Farr (two Soho swordsmiths) 'to make a very fine sword-hilt, whose beauty shall be in good workmanship and fine polish rather than an abundance of nigling work'. He continued: 'If I had 100 or 1000 hylts, that were really good work and good last I could sell them, but bad Brumigem work will not sell. We shall also want some good and some fine setts of buttons for Soho warehouse as well as a better warehouseman, as we shall have towards ye middle end of ye summer much company. Pray send me as soon as possible, two sorts of buttons for Lord Beauchamp, like those sent for Mrs Montague [Lady Mary Wortley Montague]. Good work in steel will admit of a great profit, but bad work of no profit at all. I am damn'd sick of London, but can't leave it at present.'

The attribution of the 'invention of cut-steel buttons, buckles and sword-hilts' to Boulton should receive closer attention, for these superbly attractive objects had been produced in Europe for many centuries and, indeed, the *Corpus Glossary* of *c.* 725 mentioned steel as 'a general name for certain artificially produced varieties of Iron'. Thus, the term has been in use for hundreds of years.

Thomas Gill, junior, an eminent 19th-century engineer, wrote a full description in his *Technological and Microscopic Repository* on the methods employed in the production of 'fine steel works'. There is very little other material on this subject and it is therefore advisable to make use of Gill's material, the value of which lies not only in its thoroughness but in the fact that Gill was much nearer to the period in which cut-steel was used than are any 20th-century references.

Certainly, cut-steel objects are known to have been produced in Germany or Italy since the middle of the 16th century, but these have usually served as mounts for fine portrait miniatures, cutlery and the like. Boulton may have seen these cut-steel objects, realised their potential value as attractive artifacts, and set one or many of his workmen to produce various cut-steel articles. There are indications, as mentioned earlier, that

Pair of oval pierced salt-cellars: pierced with diaper, or diamond-shaped, motifs, the pierced gallery with escutcheon for contemporary monogram.

Maker: Boulton and Fothergill, 1774.

Size: length 3¼ in, width 2½ in, height 2 in.

Weight: 1.65 oz.

Probably by Robert Adam.

Boulton had dealings with Benjamin Huntsman of Sheffield early in the former's life, and there were button-makers and stampers at Soho. The superb cut-steel sword-hilt and guard illustrated was probably a joint production of two or three specialists: the hilt would have been fashioned by Kiesel, the gold inlay on the blade by, probably, Johann Andreas Kern and the Wedgwood cameo blue and white jasperware plaques inset by one of the lapidaries employed at Soho.

No trace of Kiesel or Kern could be found until the Deutsches Klingensmuseum at Solingen, in West Germany, was contacted. This city is the cutlery centre of Germany – the counterpart, in fact, of Sheffield – and the museum's solution was obvious. Both Kiesel and Kern were itinerant swordsmiths, that is, unattached to any one master and thus probably self-taught, without even serving an apprenticeship. They engaged themselves to the highest bidder, and, having ended their commission, travelled on.

What happened to Kiesel is not known, but Kern was engaged in 1770, on Boulton's insistence, by William Matthews, in whose house Kern lodged. Kern was a master cutler specialising in gold damascening, that is, the application of beautiful gold inlay upon the blade; it is doubtful whether he ever touched the hilt, pommel or guard. Possibly, Kiesel was a cut-steel specialist, as his name sounds Scandinavian, and Swedish steelmen were masters in all sorts of craftsmanship.

Kern was discharged by Boulton in 1772, on the grounds that he was not working fast enough. This is surprising, in view of Boulton's own tendency to procrastinate in the delivery of orders. The more likely explanation for his dismissal was that being an artist and not lacking in other commissions, Kern asked for more pay and, when this was

not forthcoming, left Boulton. Kern subsequently worked for Messrs Oriel, *père et fils*, of Aldersgate Street, London. Philip Oriel was the founder of this firm, and the son was admitted to the Freedom of the Company of Stationers in 1776. (It is probable that the term stationery embraced the smaller items which might be useful to a lady or gentleman,

Plain wine funnel with a removable spigot or spout: this is enriched with a circular band of beading. The vessel is otherwise quite plain, but there is an inner circular rim, which is removable, so that it can be attached to a muslin strainer by means of a series of pierced holes. The strainer would be discarded after use.

Maker: Boulton and Fothergill, 1774.
Size: length 4½ in, diameter 2¾ in.
Weight: 2.45 oz.
Probably designed by Robert Adam.

including small swords for opening letters. Also, one may possibly absolve Boulton from any direct dealings with Kern, for whatever faults he possessed, Boulton was a great admirer of craftsmen, and it is believed that Kern's dismissal was not on his direct instructions.

In 1774, Boulton, undoubtedly feeling that he ought to extend his frontiers even further, sent a list of the articles produced at Soho to a series of London silversmiths, in spite of his dislike of the metropolis. This list is highly illuminating and, although somewhat long, is included, as it encompasses almost the whole range of Boulton's productions.

'All sorts of buttons, gilt, plated, platina, steel, inlaid, both of yellow metal, and superfine buttons of various colours, and with foil. Women's and men's chains of steel, and inlaid with gold, or with gilt metals, or quite common ones. Men's and women's gilt chains from the most common to the most fine ones, and with cameos and different colours. All manner of silver and silver plated articles such as tea kitchens, bread baskets, candlesticks, waiters; all sorts of vases, mounted in strong gilt or ormulu, geographical and astronomical clocks, also clocks upon a construction quite new, having but one wheel in them. Gilt glass and filigree trinkets and steel sword-hilts, all sorts of sleeve buttons, viz., platina, steel, inlaid, tortoiseshell, plain and inlaid boxes, instrument cases, toothpick cases, sundry articles in silver filigree, in shagreen, chapes of all qualities and sorts, and sundry more articles. Besides the hardware commissioned goods, we also serve our friends in Staffordshire earthenware pottery, factored from Wedgwood's potteries at Etruria, "to the best advantage".'

There was a plethora of correspondence flowing from Birmingham to Etruria – that is, from Boulton to his friend, Wedgwood – and one might ponder on the paucity of letters received in return. While Boulton was constantly making plans, ordering cream earthenware for factoring cameo jasperware, Wedgwood was, in contrast, most reticent: of the thirty or so letters in the Wedgwood Box at the Birmingham Assay Office, most are concerned with Wedgwood's alarm that the Act prohibiting Irish imports might be defeated, and he devoted much of his time towards furthering this cause. Boulton and Wedgwood must have met frequently however at the Lunar Society, and it was within that convivial atmosphere that they exchanged reports and views. There was, perhaps, little need for the busy potter to write to Boulton.

In 1775 Boulton must have felt the lack of a specialist head of department for his plating establishment, and he approached William Hancock, an eminent Sheffield craftsman. Boulton offered him regular employment and a house, or part of a house, for himself and his wife, along with other inducements. The reply from Hancock was favourable and in October, Boulton sent a letter, written in his own hand (and not scratched by a clerk), saying: 'I think you had better bring Mrs Hancock along with you . . . in all matters you will find me disposed to render your situation agreeable and comfortable.'

Another silversmith arrived at Soho in 1775. Boulton was approached by George Wyon, a member of the family of celebrated medallists, who sent a recommendation for James Watt, silversmith – not to be confused with James Watt, the engineer. 'Watt', stated Wyon, 'is known to his namesake.' Indeed, James Watt, the silversmith, became a head of department and was still working in 1782. He is mentioned here because a noted writer claimed some time ago that the famous James Watt had fashioned a punch-ladle; indeed, with his genius for invention, he could have made one, but did not. It was just one of those misunderstandings caused by identical names, which historians dread.

By this time, Boulton had increased both staff and output, but he continued to use delaying excuses with his clients or to refuse outright to fill an order if he was reluctant, for one reason or another. In reply to a letter from Warwick, Boulton said: 'Fish trowels

Dining room at Osterley Park, which Robert
Adam started to design in 1761. (The candelabra
on the mantelpiece are Boulton articles.)

19 years. Also, he was engaged to work at Syon and at Alnwick Castle. Syon must have
been the main work for a considerable period, since Adam was not engaged upon
Northumberland House until 1770. Richard Warner, the antiquary, in his *Tour of 1802*,
said that £200,000 was spent on restoring Alnwick, and this enormous sum is quite
credible, considering Adam's style and method of work. Also in 1761, Adam designed
a fine bridge for Sir Nathaniel Curzon, afterwards Lord Scarsdale, at Kedlestone
Derbyshire.

Adam received the formal appointment of Architect to King George III, an elevated
position which he resigned on being elected a Member of Parliament for his home con-
stituency of Kinross, in 1768. He designed ceilings for the Queen's House, still visible
until Nash's reconstruction of Buckingham House, later to become Buckingham Palace,
between 1825–7. The motifs which Robert Adam used in his buildings are found also
in his furniture designs, as one sees in the furniture at Moor Park in Hertfordshire.
Originally built between 1720 and 1739, by Sir James Thornhill and the Venetian

architect Giacomo Leoni, the house had added wings designed by Adam. He did not allow 'Athenian' Stuart to outshine him in the adaptation of Grecian motifs, since many of the houses which Adam built for his clients were of the same idiom, with impressive pediments, Ionic columns and Grecian friezes. Study of his furniture will illustrate how Adam's Greco-Italian studies influenced his silver designs.

A console table by Adam for Sir Robert Dundas, the owner of Moor Park, is a superb example. True, it has festoons of foliage, but these are light, and enrich the support of the half-oval chamfered marble top, the frieze of which is well supported on three lambs' head splaying legs, curling down to well carved hooves. The Pompeiian temple influence is well visible here, as in a fine armchair, also from Moor Park, which is decorated with shell and foliate motifs and rosette bosses. The frieze supporting the seat bears a central artificial shell-and-scroll motif, running towards figures of Minerva, and the feet are claw-and-ball. A sofa, probably from the same suite, is similarly enriched.

Arthur T. Bolton's magnificent work on Robert and James Adam illustrates various specimens of classical furniture. There are two side-tables by William Kent, who also studied Palladian and Roman architecture, and whose work, although popular at the time, now seems to lack grace. (These tables were at Devonshire House.) They are wanting in Adam's lightness and elegance of conception.

At Kedlestone House, Adam permitted himself palm ornament on a delightfully conceived mirror, the finial incorporating the owner's coat-of-arms, and with the whole topped by a cruciform spray of artificial foliage. The state bedroom has a magnificent four-poster bed, the columns of which are also palm motif. There is a lamp pedestal formed as a tapering console, embellished with intertwining floral swags, and flower-head bosses in the centre; the pediment has a typical Adam festoon, with a flowerhead boss, and the frieze is composed of ogees and scrolls. The pedestal was intended to serve as a stand for a Boulton ormulu and Blue John candelabrum, the whole on an in-curving marble plinth standing on three ormulu ball feet.

A chimney-piece by Adam represented a Grecian temple, with Ionic scrolls at either side of the friezed pediment and delicately carved foliate swags with a goddess's mask in the centre. The frieze around the scrolls illustrated the egg-and-tongue motif.

Adam's theories advanced: a curtain cornice was to have palm-leaf embellishment; a pair of bronze lamp pedestals were to embody all the classical features of Pompeii, with harpies supporting the lamp standard, which itself bore a grotesque mask; and the twin candle holders were in turn enriched with further grotesqueries. The terminals were cherubs sitting in niches, one pedestal surmounted by a warrior, the other by a small sitting faun.

A harpsicord which Adam designed for the Empress Catherine of Russia was developed from a Pompeiian ceiling, with rectangular panels, and friezes of ovoids and floral bosses at each corner. An oval panel in the centre was embellished by swags of light foliage and darts, and musical instruments. The frieze around the oval panel was composed of false acanthus foliage, and there was a musical-arrangement motif – a lyre and crossed trumpets – in the centre. The central horizontal panel depicted the Muses playing upon their lyres, and the whole was further enriched with delicate swags and festoons, also embellished with musical instruments. The supports were caryatid harpies holding festoons, reclining upon a vase-type standard. In the very centre of the base-board was the Empress's elaborate carved coat-of-arms.

Adam's designs continued to echo Pompeii. A table top for Osterley, dated 1775, could have come straight from Italy: palm foliage in heart-shaped cartouches formed the frieze. Flowerheads linked by harpies enclosed in light floral swags towards a panelled circular boss formed the top, which was of white marble with lilac, green and blue inlay.

Adam also gradually introduced Etruscan motifs into his schemes, and the Roman liking for ovoid-enriched panels. Chair-arms made to represent eagles and chair-backs illustrating vases or lyres lent themselves to Adam's thesis of enrichment and extended his repertoire of classical motifs. He produced designs for hanging-lamps in bronze and, presumably, in ormulu. Again, these harked back to Pompeiian styles, with dolphin figures for clock-cases, Minerva-like draped figures and spreading vases tipped by flame finials, placed on harpy supports.

An inkstand, designed for Sir William Watkins Wynn's house in St James's Square, c. 1773, was a most elaborately conceived object. Cast and gilt bronze or ormulu* cherubs supported an urn-shaped inkpot, enriched with masks, swags, and festoons

Robert Adam design for a chimney board for the Etruscan dressing room at Osterley Park. The sketch, dated 1777, shows several of the classical motifs used by the designer in much of his work.

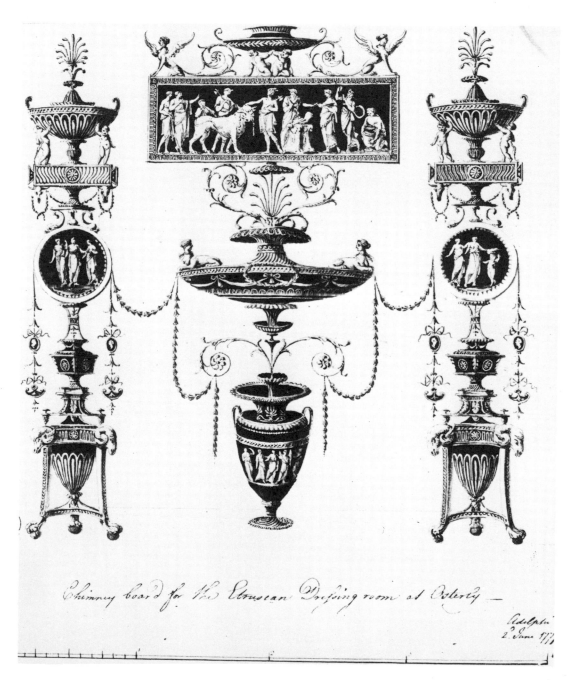

Chimney board for the Etruscan Dressing room at Osterly —

Adelphi
2 June 17

Silverwire sweetmeat basket.
Maker: Boulton and Fothergill, dated 1774.
Size: width 6½ in, height 2 in, length 7½ in.
Weight: 6.01 oz.
This article was probably designed by Adam.
Left
An épergne: these dishes were intended to enrich a table with fruit, nuts, etc. It is fully described on pp. 79–80. See marks, below.
Maker: Matthew Boulton, dated 1790.
Size: height 12 in, width 8½ in, diameter of bowl 12 in.
Weight: 55.14 oz.
Probably of Adam design.

vine leaf and grape motifs. The base is a solid vessel with a collet, or incurving, oval rim, also enriched with a twisted heavy wire, and the swing handle is of a similar type, with a three-lugged hinge at either side; because Adam usually designed elaborate silver, and this article is comparatively plain, certain identification is very difficult. It is known, for instance, that Boulton would borrow interesting articles from clients for copying – he borrowed a cassolette from Lady Mary Wortley Montague – and there is therefore no certain way of identifying the designer of this article.

A magnificent Boulton cream-ewer dated 1785, on a cast circular base, of massive-gauge silver, with a heavy reeded rib and a reeded rim, is extant. The plain D-shaped handle rises from the ewer, on a cast circular base, and is attached to the body by a 'trumpet' union. There is a contemporary cypher. Another Boulton and Fothergill piece, a salver, dated 1774, bears a strong Adam influence: the central plate is quite plain but for a contemporary lightly-engraved coat-of-arms beneath engraved flower-head festoons. The cast and pierced border is enriched with husk festoons and inverted palm leaves. No feet are visible, but it is assumed that these existed to lift the heavy salver off the table. An absolutely breath-taking wine ewer by Boulton and Fothergill,

Superbly conceived 'ewer' wine-jug: see p. 87.
Maker: Boulton and Fothergill, 1776.
Size: height 12 in, diameter at base 3½ in.
Weight: 21.54 oz.
Designed by Robert Adam.

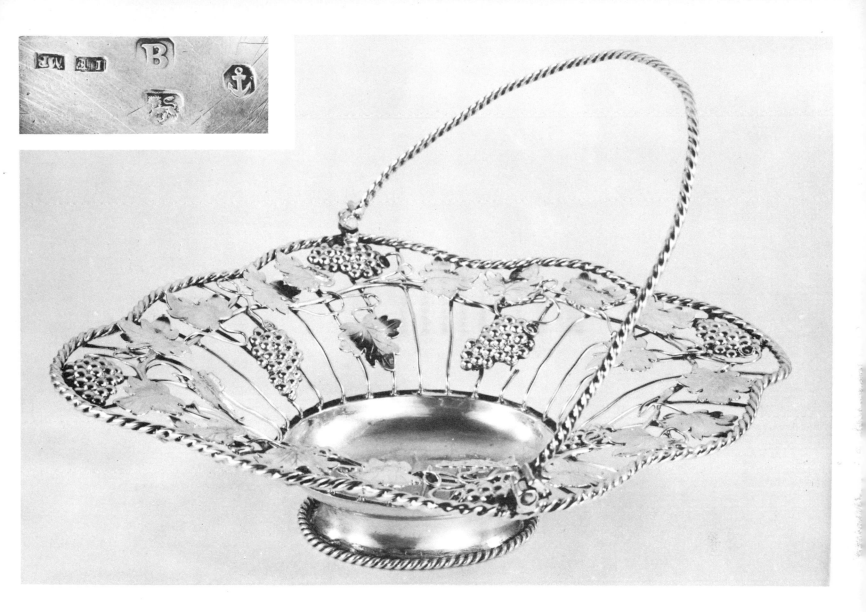

Silverwire sweetmeat basket.
Maker: Boulton and Fothergill, dated 1774.
Size: width 6½ in, height 2 in, length 7½ in.
Weight: 6.01 oz.
This article was probably designed by Adam.
Left
An épergne: these dishes were intended to enrich a table with fruit, nuts, etc. It is fully described on pp. 79–80. See marks, below.
Maker: Matthew Boulton, dated 1790.
Size: height 12 in, width 8½ in, diameter of bowl 12 in.
Weight: 55.14 oz.
Probably of Adam design.

vine leaf and grape motifs. The base is a solid vessel with a collet, or incurving, oval rim, also enriched with a twisted heavy wire, and the swing handle is of a similar type, with a three-lugged hinge at either side; because Adam usually designed elaborate silver, and this article is comparatively plain, certain identification is very difficult. It is known, for instance, that Boulton would borrow interesting articles from clients for copying – he borrowed a cassolette from Lady Mary Wortley Montague – and there is therefore no certain way of identifying the designer of this article.

A magnificent Boulton cream-ewer dated 1785, on a cast circular base, of massive-gauge silver, with a heavy reeded rib and a reeded rim, is extant. The plain D-shaped handle rises from the ewer, on a cast circular base, and is attached to the body by a 'trumpet' union. There is a contemporary cypher. Another Boulton and Fothergill piece, a salver, dated 1774, bears a strong Adam influence: the central plate is quite plain but for a contemporary lightly-engraved coat-of-arms beneath engraved flower-head festoons. The cast and pierced border is enriched with husk festoons and inverted palm leaves. No feet are visible, but it is assumed that these existed to lift the heavy salver off the table. An absolutely breath-taking wine ewer by Boulton and Fothergill,

Superbly conceived 'ewer' wine-jug: see p. 87.
Maker: Boulton and Fothergill, 1776.
Size: height 12 in, diameter at base 3 ½ in.
Weight: 21.54 oz.
Designed by Robert Adam.

Cut-steel dress sword hilt: decorated by Kern *c.* 1760–70. The sword is more fully described on p. 54. The cameo and white jasperware plaques on the hilt of the sword are thought to have been designed by Flaxman and produced by Wedgwood.

The figure appearing on the knuckle-guard is that of Victory; at the base of the hilt, a Maenad, or woman in Bacchic ecstasy, who formed part of the train of Dionysus; and on the guard (horizontally), the poet Aeschylus.

A Chester-made mazerine: this item is file-pierced and may have been produced by a local silversmith. It is engraved with contemporary arms and motto.
Maker: Boulton and Fothergill, dated 1769 and with Chester hall-marks.
Size: diameter 12 in.
Weight: 22 oz 5 dwt.
A 'spool-shaped' dish-warmer. It has a contemporary crest and motto.
Maker: Boulton and Fothergill, dated 1773.

Furthermore, there is the superbly enriched cassolette illustrated, namely a perfume or perfumed pastille burner, used to fumigate a sick-room or dining-room. This beautiful article, at Temple Newsam House, Leeds, was made by Boulton and Fothergill, and is dated 1779. The vase-shaped body has an appliqué star-oval medallion, and cast appliqué festoons; the base is enriched with acanthus foliage and a rim of beading. The upper frieze is of a scroll type, and the whole is supported by three harpies on splaying legs, terminating in claw-and-ball feet. There is no base-plate, but soldered straps, also embellished with light guilloche ornament, take the form of inverted additional supports. The legs are pinned to ball-shaped ebony-wood balusters, presumably to preserve the table-top from being scorched. The lift-out lid is superlatively pierced in diaper, or diamond-shaped, enrichment and is surmounted by a spool-shaped finial, topped by a baluster of acanthus foliage.

A recipe for a cassolette in H. W. Lewer's *A Book of Simples* (published by Sampson Low, Mauston & Co., London, 1908) states: 'To make a perfume to burn in a chamber: take benjamin, storax and labdanum, of each a like, a little damaske powder, orace powder a little, a little frankensense and mirr powder of Jewpiter. Beat all these together to a paste in a hot mortar and to make it up in the fashion of great black cloves & to burn them when you please its a pleasant smell.' Richard Thomlinson's *Medicinal Dispensatory of 1657*, which was a translation of Jean de Renou's Parisian *Dispensatorium Galeno-chimicum*, published in 1608, stated 'put in a brazen or silver pot which the vulgar call a cassolet'.

This list of Adam-inspired articles is nearly at a close, but there are some more items to be taken into consideration. One of the colour plates on page 41 shows a pair of oval Boulton and Fothergill sauce tureens, dated 1773. These have fluted lids, enriched with mock-acanthus floral motifs around the friezes, ribbon-and-wreath mounts on the bodies, and cast appliqué ornament, with intertwining flowerheads in scrollwork. The handles of ribbon-and-wreath motif are cast to the bodies. The finials on the lids are formed as acanthus buds. These tureens are finely engraved with contemporary cyphers and arms.

Another Adam-style item is an ingenious dish-warmer, somewhat similar to the Irish dish-rings, but although it is formed as a spool-shaped circlet, the piercing and cast motifs, especially the ribbon-and-wreath borders by now associated with Adam's work, point to his own design work. There is a four-light spirit heater in the centre, supported on four reeded straps, in an oval cartouche, forming a gimbel, so that the lamp can be used for both the top and bottom of the ring. The top and bottom are of different diameters, to accommodate different sized plates. There is a well-turned yew-wood handle, which is engraved at the union to the body with a contemporary crest and initial. The article is by Boulton and Fothergill, dated 1773.

Adam's work for other people

Boulton's stratagem of making excuses to refuse or delay unwelcome work has been mentioned in an earlier chapter, with particular reference to his dealings with Lady Norton. This prospective customer had been sent to him by James Wyatt with a commission for a pair of three-branched candelabra on triangular bases, but Boulton refused the order, using Wyatt to pass the message on. He may have believed that if he would not produce an article, neither would any of his rivals, but in this case his self-confidence was proved wrong.

A pair of fine candelabra of exactly this type is illustrated in a sale catalogue of 1946, but these items, dated 1774, were made by John Carter of London. (All catalogues mentioned in this chapter are for Sotheby's sales.) Certainly, the illustration and description of the candelabra reveal that they were modelled in a style requiring a great deal of time and craftsmanship, which may have prompted Boulton's refusal to make a similar pair. The inverted tricorn bases have bands of scrolling foliage, and are on stepped plinths; the centre of the base-plate has a cast flowerhead in a circlet of beading, and the splaying reeded supports (surmounted by rams' heads) are placed within top and bottom straps of ogees. The branches are mock-acanthus scrolls, and the vase-capital is topped by a spool-shaped feather-acanthus motif, the whole being surmounted by a pine-cone finial.

There is a footnote in the catalogue: 'The owner's London house was in St James's Square, the residence having many fittings and furnishings designed by Robert Adam, and in view of the proportions of the candelabra and the quality of the chasing, it is not unlikely that this lot was designed by Adam.' It is heartening to note the cataloguer's diffidence, because unless signed designs remain extant, there is no proof that these superb articles were designed by Robert Adam. The owner of the house was none other than Sir William Watkins Wynn, for whom Adam had indeed designed the house in St James's Square.

There were other users of Adam motifs, as well; John Carter, it would appear, worked from Adam designs, as did, of course, Hester Bateman and Parker and Wakelin, who commissioned candelabra from Boulton. It could well be that an oval dessert basket and stand by Wakelin and Taylor, being post-Adam, dated 1797, were imitated in the Adam style by James Wyatt, and it is possible that Andrew Fogelberg and Stephen Gilbert also worked in Adam motifs, with festoons and appliqué medallions. A sale catalogue of 1966 showed a superb vase-shaped tea urn on an incurving triangular plinth with a fluted border and a bright-cut centre. The body was supported by three female bust-and-claw terminals, and was chased with palm leaves and shallow flutes, with three lion's-mask spouts, and ivory and silver loop taps. There was a fluted border, the beaded rim hinged to two rising handles, while the lobed cover was topped with a pine-cone and foliate motif finial. This article was made by Daniel Smith and Richard Sharp, London, 1783, and was twenty inches high.

The same sale contained a beautiful boat-shaped inkstand on four palm-foliage bracket feet. The handles were of the sweeping harp type, and the sides were pierced with scrolls, with an applied beaded rim above. The centre had three partly fluted vases with domed covers and ball finials. This was wrought by John Tayleur of London, 1786. Both the above mentioned items were in the Adam style.

Another sale catalogue for May 1967 contains a most superb oval tea-caddy enriched with two beaded bands enclosing scrolls and husk decoration on a matted ground. The slightly-domed crested cover had similar chased scrollwork and a hinged ring finial. The stand, also with beaded borders, rested on four tapered column supports surmounted by ram's-head masks with laurel festoons between. This caddy was by Fogelberg and Gilbert, London, 1785. The epitome of Adam enrichment was shown in the same sale: a punch bowl by Thomas Heming, London, 1771, was offered. From the rams' masks to the foliate and festoon enrichment, this was based on Adam design: oddly enough, this bowl, like the tricorn candelabra, belonged to Sir William Watkins Wynn.

In the same year, 1967, another catalogue, for April, illustrates a most unusual Irish vase-shaped hotwater jug by John Lloyd of Dublin, c. 1775. The vessel was on a circular collet foot enriched with anthemion leaves, and a wire of heavy beading, rising on a spool-shaped collet to feather-acanthus appliqué foliage on the lower part of the jug, and with festoons of pendant drapery around the body. The neck was composed of heavy fluting, and had a band of coarse beading to support it, and this motif was repeated on the neck, which had a hinged cover, topped with a pine-cone finial. The contemporary handle was of boxwood. The jug stood 12½ inches high, and its weight was 34.18 ounces.

The neo-classical designers were not content to rely solely on Adam. A sale catalogue of January 1967 illustrates a pair of fine parcel-gilt ewers (the term parcel-gilt indicates partial gilding) by Thomas Heming, London, 1777, which might have come from an Adam design, but was probably influenced by designs of Sir William Hamilton, the British Ambassador at Naples, who, in 1766, published a one-volume work entitled *Collection of Etruscan, Greek and Roman Antiquities*. The full-bellied bodies of the vessels were chased with delicate bands of anthemion motifs on matted grounds, and at the necks with tapered lobes pendant from interlaced ribbon work, with reeded high loop handles, and on small circular bases chased with bands of beaded ornament. Sir William Hamilton was the husband of Emma, the mistress of Admiral Lord Nelson. A painting in the London National Portrait Gallery depicts Hamilton as a presentable gentleman perusing a large tome illustrating what appear to be Etruscan motifs, while, behind him, on a William Kent-style table stands an Etruscan-enriched ewer.

Another neo-classical vessel appears in a sale catalogue of November 1966. This was a large hotwater jug by Daniel Smith and Robert Sharp, and it may have derived from the Adam influence. The body was hexagonal and enriched with half flutes on the lower part of the vessel. The upper part was quite plain and the hexagonal base and rim of the domed cover were reeded. The lid was of the flap-hinge type, surmounted by a heavy baluster knop, and the boxwood handle rose upwards from a reeded union at the base of the body. The height was 12 inches.

Adam, it seems, would not commit his designs to one silversmith; he accepted commissions from any eminent craftsman, for he designed a superlative six-piece tea service for his friend David Garrick, which was produced by James Young and Orlando Jackson of London, in 1774. The motif is typically Adam. The tea urn, coffee pot and the teapot have swags of appliqué drapery broken by flowerhead bands just beneath the beaded lids, and the bodies are composed of alternating straps of fluting and matt-chasing. All the pieces are on circular anthemion-enriched bases. The urn and the teapot are egg-shaped, the jugs vase-shaped, and the two slop basins almost hemispherical. The coffee pot and the milk jug have rising fluted covers surmounted with flame finials, while the large tea urn is on a square pedestal enriched with beading and appliqué oval flowerhead panels, and stands on scrolling florally-enriched feet. The basins or slop bowls have twisted wire handles.

In 1783 Adam designed a magnificent twelve-piece silver-gilt toilet service for Lady Craven. It will be recalled that she was also a customer of Boulton. All the pieces were enriched with husk festoons and ribbon ties, and alternating various foliate motifs. The most important embellishment is on the pair of large rectangular boxes, repoussé with classical mythological scenes. The service was wrought by Daniel Smith and Robert Sharp. It would be possible to cite many more items from Robert Adam's repertoire, but over-emphasis might defeat the purpose; what has been attempted is to give an adequate illustration of the versatility of this great designer, and to show the extent of his influence on other silversmiths.

After studying the actual designs in such detail, it becomes necessary to elaborate on the silversmiths' work which these demanded. The *cire perdue*, or lost-wax process is described in *Silver Boxes*, and Cellini's method was also carefully explained. Of course, Adam and his followers, as architects, were adept modellers in clay and terracotta, and it was from these models that the vessels, candlesticks and boxes were cast, The motifs were modelled by the designers, and the finishing touches applied by the silversmiths, chiefly the matt-chasing and the repoussé enrichment. This process is also described in *Silver Boxes*.

It will be recalled that a hollow vessel can be produced in two ways: one, by hand-raising, or hammering an ingot of silver from the flat into a hollow container, and then applying the enrichment, either cast or repoussé; the other, by casting the whole vessel.

This is a much more skilled and laborious way, but Cellini managed it, as did many other craftsmen, by creating a wax or moist sand core and casting the whole vessel from it, the outside surface included, with full embellishments. Since Boulton commissioned various craftsmen, it is probable that the silver manufactory could produce hand-raised articles. There were also chasers to apply the ornament, and casters to attach the appliqué motifs to the sides, as well as piercers to perforate the intricately designed motifs.

The more sophisticated silversmiths had rolling-mills by the 1780s and could make sheets of thin malleable silver which could be made up to any desired commission. The Bateman family, in particular, took advantage of this rolled silver, and thus many articles from Hester Bateman's workshop are thin in gauge. It was a simple matter to roll out a strip of silver, shape it to the required design, and solder it together.

James Wyatt

There are no short cuts to learning: Anthony Dale in *James Wyatt, Architect*, stated that Wyatt visited Italy, arriving eventually at Venice in 1762, after a period of four years spent at Rome studying architecture with great thoroughness. (He lay on his back in a very precarious position while he studied the void of the dome of St Peter's, and spent hours in the Pantheon, so that he could draw and measure every portion.) Finally he studied under Marco Antonio Vincenzi at Venice. Vincenzi revived Michelangelesque motifs, and worked in various Italian churches.

Wyatt probably returned to England in 1766, having imbibed deeply the Greco-Italian style of architecture, and was elected an Associate of the Royal Academy in 1770. It has been said that Wyatt's mansions were a distinct advance on the work of his predecessors, although his houses had a certain sameness in their outward appearance. The same charge could be levelled at Adam and James 'Athenian' Stuart.

There were critics of Adam who placed Stuart and Wyatt on pedestals and attempted to dethrone the master, in the late 1770s. Much is made of the rivalry between the brothers Adam and James Wyatt. If this existed – and was not just manufactured by rival factions – it would have been an entirely natural phenomenon. The Adams had been part of the pioneering of neo-classicism and did not take kindly to an inventive youth, brilliant though he might be. It took the Adams twenty years to overcome their dislike of Wyatt.

Wyatt gradually became an authority on Gothic architecture, or rather, Gothic-revival enrichment, and it will be recalled that he Gothicised part of Westminster Abbey at the time of the Handel Commemorative Concerts. It is not surprising that the Adam brothers might have regarded Wyatt as an interloper, for he was commissioned by Sir William Watkins Wynn, to re-design the south elevation of Wynnstay, which Adam had designed in 1772. Eminence appeared to pursue Wyatt: in 1785, he became a Royal Academician, and in 1805, at the express wish of the King, became the President of the Royal Academy, but this was an empty appointment, since his election was not ratified by the royal signature.

What was James Wyatt's connection with Boulton? Horace Walpole, fourth Earl of Orford (1717–97), author, wit and a letter writer, was originally a great admirer of Robert Adam, and complained in 1773, that Wyatt had stolen Adam's designs, so the conclusion must arise that Wyatt was working as an architect in the early 1770s. Wyatt's association with Boulton's silverwork is illustrated by James Wyatt's own house in Foley Place, Portland Place, where the ornamental frieze running along the elevation of the house almost exactly duplicated the guilloche motif which Adam continually used, and this would appear to indicate that Wyatt had also seen the Pompeiian motifs when he was in Italy.

Horace Walpole eventually quarrelled with Adam, and attacked him very subtly through a pamphlet written under a pseudonym by Robert Smirke, the painter, who was himself a mischievous critic, and who was eventually employed by Wyatt to paint subjects for chimney-pieces. There is a pair of torchères, or pedestals for lamps, at Kenwood House which were designed by Wyatt for the Etruscan room at Heveningham Hall, *c.* 1780–4. They are of carved wood, painted in the form of urns standing on pedestals of square section; painted in the Etruscan style in terracotta and black with figures and ornament on a green ground. This motif might have been by Smirke. The Etruscan room at Heveningham Hall was completed by Wyatt before 1784 for Sir Gerrard Vanneck; the room and its furniture was painted by Biago Rebecca, who also painted the ceiling panels in the entrance hall at Kenwood House.

Wyatt became the pet of the dilettanti connoisseurs, and one of Wyatt's pupils named Hunt, writing in 1827, stated that twelve noblemen combined to allow a fixed sum every year to Wyatt, so that he might have an independent income and not accept the invitation of the Empress Catherine to go to Russia. Young Wyatt's election to the Royal Academy in 1770 made the exclusion of Robert Adam extraordinary.

The Etruscan room at Heveningham Hall, designed by James Wyatt before 1784.

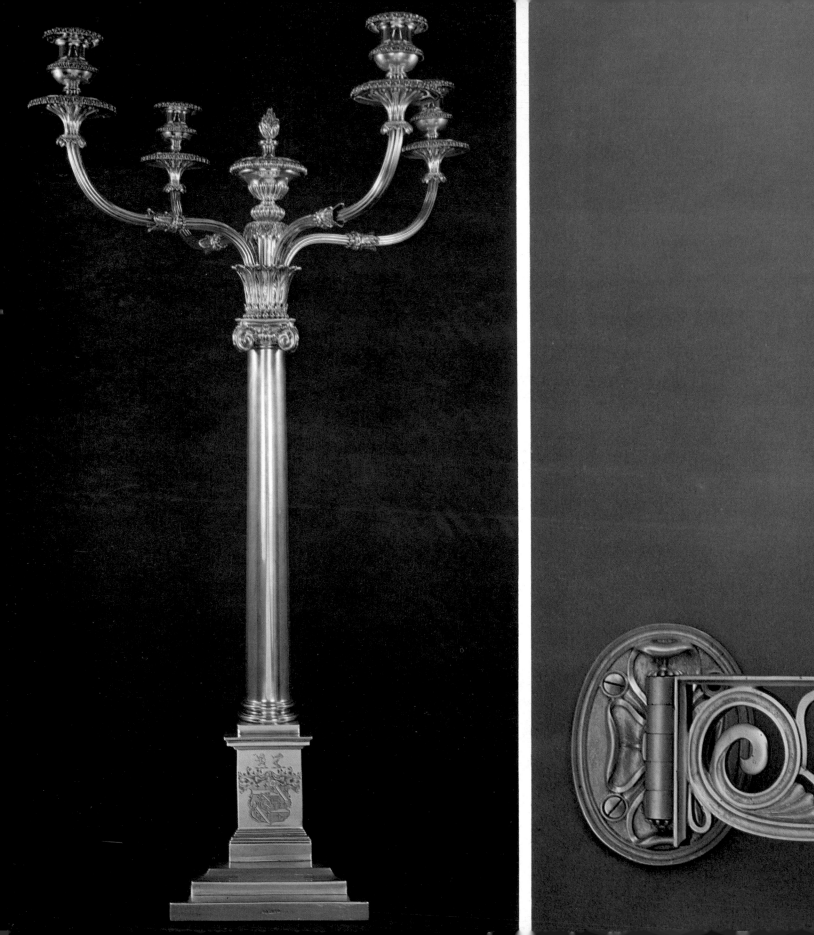

A pair of large Blue John ormulu-mounted ewers: the spouts formed as gilt ormulu satyr masks, with large double-scroll ormulu chased gilt handles. The lips fluted and divided by circular collet rims and terminating in laurel-motif rims. The bases formed as upward-fluting trumpet-shaped pedestals, surmounted with anthemion foliage at the union with the Blue John bodies, and with laurel-leaf motifs on the square massive bases, c. 1765–75.

Size: height including the handle 17 in, base 4 in. square.

Note: neither of the ewers is marked, and it is firmly believed that few pieces of ormulu were marked, either by Boulton or Wedgwood; however, it is dangerous to generalise, and if there are any marked pieces, they might bear 'MB' or 'JW' in skeleton-letters, namely, letters struck in separate punches.

engine undefined; it might take months of work before the engine would be working at full pressure. It is probable that one of the partners supervised the assembly of the early engines, and they made their income by charging a premium amounting to one-third of the savings in fuel made by their engine as compared with a common one. The engine business increased and Boulton and Watt engaged William Murdoch, the famous engineer, in 1777, to superintend the assembly of the engines, as well as to put his attention to experimentation in gas lighting. In 1782, Watt patented the rotative engine, and two years later obtained a further patent on a parallel motion device for guiding the piston rods to supplement the former. The engine business had, indeed, become a successful venture.

The first mention of the great James Watt appears in the letter-books, when on 21 April 1773, Fothergill wrote to Boulton: 'I was in hopes Mr Watt would have din'd with me today as I could have informed you relating the engin, however, I now hear the new steem valves answers extremely well and that the wheel engine will be ready for tryal next week, perhaps you may have further information by this conveyance from Mr Scales, to whom I mentioned your desires last night.'

All the members of the Lunar Society supported Watt's partnership with Boulton, and in August 1773, two-thirds of the invention passed to Boulton. On 17 May 1774, Watt and his two children set out for Birmingham, where Boulton had installed them in Newhall Park. In March 1777, they moved to Regent's Park, Harper's Hill, which was only a short distance from Soho. Watt's first wife, Margaret, had died in 1773, and in the summer of 1776, Watt married Ann McGregor of Glasgow, in what could have been only a marriage of convenience, for while she took care of him and his children as well as her own, she was a nagging wife, and it appears that he was a henpecked husband.

Watt was awarded many honorary degrees and fellowships, but declined with dignity the offer of a baronetcy from the Prime Minister, Lord Liverpool. Watt's greatest honour came when, in 1814, he was elected one of the eight foreign associates of the French Academy.

It has been said that wealth brought Watt peace of mind, serenity and wisdom; recognition gave him immense dignity and presence, which was yet modest, without pride or pretension. The remainder of his life-story was one of mounting success, and he died in 1819 at Heathfield Hall, near Birmingham, which was designed for him by Samuel Wyatt.

As so much honour was bestowed upon Watt, it is surprising that Boulton, while attaining civic honours, never attained equal rank, for it was the partnership which had brought about Watt's fame.

The end of the Boulton-Fothergill partnership

At the same time that Watt and Boulton were busily developing the steam engine, Boulton was also at the height of production in the silverware manufactory, and found himself extended financially on all fronts. Although his numerous projects prospered, he had to work very hard. His widespread responsibilities perhaps hardened his attitude towards John Fothergill, who had never shared with him the full burden of planning and financing, and quickly got out of his depth when times were difficult.

Ironically, it was just at this time that Fothergill seems to have realised the immense potential of Watt's invention, and seen in the man himself a threat to his own partnership with Boulton. In June 1780, he offered to stand as joint guarantor for funds needed to start the engine business, and wrote: 'If you can borrow the £4,000, for twenty years on personal security, I shall very gladly join you therein.' Fothergill continued in the same letter, with the claim that he too had subsidised Watt and Kier in the past, as if to remind Boulton that he was owed something in return – presumably a share in the profits of the steam engine enterprise. There are no records of a reply from his partner.

Boulton and Watt were much better suited to each other in temperament, and worked together in mutual trust and understanding. Fothergill was gradually ousted from his position at the manufactory, but not without a struggle. Boulton and Watt tried to get legal assistance in the affair, but as no real legal partnership existed between the former and Fothergill, the law was no solution. Subsequently, three men, Vere, Foreman, and Garbett, who were all known to both parties, were asked to act as arbitrators, but nothing was formally resolved. Finally, after five or six years' dissension, Fothergill died, in 1782. Boulton continued to pay his former partner's widow a pension of about £300 per annum, from 1782 until 1791. He also helped place Fothergill's two sons in careers, one with the East India Company, and the other with the Bank of England. He took a kindly interest in their affairs, and also remained close to Fothergill's daughter.

Although he never had a perfect relationship with John Fothergill, Boulton obviously liked one of the sons, William. Indeed, the latter seems to have had a much stronger character than Boulton's own son, Matty. He distinguished himself in naval service, and his citation for 'action off the Cape of Good Hope' in September 1799 was addressed to Matthew Boulton. He must have valued the older man's approval highly. It is strange that the disparity of character between Fothergill and Boulton should have been mirrored in their sons, in reverse.

Blue John feldspar

At about the time that James Watt was first a guest of Boulton's at Soho, the latter was becoming interested in incorporating Blue John, or blue fluor feldspar in certain objects. On 28 December 1768, he wrote to John Whitehurst (the horologist who has been discussed as a member of the Lunar Society), saying that he was in urgent need of an assaying balance and hoped that the work upon it was advanced. He further asked Whitehurst not to delay the dispatch, as his laboratory was finished, and he would soon be in a position to begin his operations. Also, he had found a use for 'Blew John' and would be obliged if Whitehurst would find out for him whether the mine which contained this feldspar was available or leased to another manufacturer. If leased, would Whitehurst inquire when it would be available again, as Boulton wanted to lease it for a year. Finally, he implored Whitehurst to remember to send him a map of Derbyshire.

There followed a voluminous correspondence between Whitehurst, Boulton, Darwin and Small to Johann Jacob Ferber, a Swedish geologist working in Germany. Ferber was full of praise for Whitehurst, to whom he had been recommended by Benjamin Franklin, and cited Dr Small as his instructor on the Derbyshire method of making porcelain. It is curious, however, that his *Sections of Derbyshire Strata*, published in 1776 is remarkably like Whitehurst's book, which was published two years later.

One might briefly examine the mineral, or rather minerals, which constitute Derbyshire feldspar. Since the subject calls for specialist knowledge, John Mawe's work on the subject will be freely quoted. Mawe stated that there were two mines, in the mountains, which produced that beautiful compact fluor, Blue John, which was found in pipe, or horizontal, veins. Usually the pieces were only about three or four inches thick, or smaller, but there were others with one strong vein which displayed a geographical figure, like a coloured map. Very occasionally, pieces were found a foot thick, and these were the most rare and valuable. The colouring matter was generally thought to be iron, although it might have been asphalt containing pyrites in a decomposed state. Mawe listed twelve chief varieties of the feldspar (details of which are given in Appendix V) and, as a footnote to his discussion, added: 'Messrs

Brown and Company, the proprietors, are happy to show travellers their manufactory, and give them every information. Their wholesale warehouse is in Tavistock Street, Covent Garden, and exhibits the greatest variety of elegantly turned vases, urns etc., formed of this beautiful stone, at the same price as at the manufactory; also the most beautiful and extensive collection of minerals in the kingdom.' This interesting information implies that Boulton was not alone in producing Blue John items, but had competitors, although the period which Mawe discussed was slightly later than the Boulton era.

François Amié Argand

Argand's lamp attracted Boulton's attention because of its beauty. There is a drawing of such a lamp in one of Boulton's pattern-books, and on delving into the biography of the inventor, a tale of tragedy bordering almost on the ludicrous is revealed.

François Amié Argand was born in Geneva in July 1750. His family concerned itself with silversmithing, horology and jewellery-making. Argand left Geneva in 1775 and, against his father's wishes that he should enter the clergy, applied himself to science and a study of physics and chemistry. During these studies, Argand became interested in distillation, and his experiments and improvements in this field attracted the wine-growers of Languedoc. He demonstrated his inventions to the Royal Academy of Sciences of Montpellier in 1780 and emerged with Royal decorations and 120,000 *livres* from the province. While experimenting with distillation, Argand conceived a new form of wick for oil lamps which would add greatly to the light given, improving upon the smoking and smelly lamps of the time. Argand proceeded to take out a provisional patent for a limited period only, the cost of this being considerably less than for a full patent. The Argand lamp was patented in London on 12 March 1784, although on 22 February it had already been advertised for sale in the *Journal de Paris*.

Argand was introduced to Boulton by William Parker, a Birmingham general merchant and glass-blower, in February 1784. Boulton was obviously struck with the ingenuity of the principle of the lamp, and agreed to manufacture it, but made no great effort to assist Argand to patent it. When the provisional patent lapsed in 1786, Boulton continued to manufacture the lamp, but without sole monopoly.

It is an inescapable conclusion that Boulton treated Argand very badly, but his other enterprises may have taken up more of his interest. He had by this time met James Watt, and the engine business was prospering. Also, the Cornish tin mines were working full spate. It is possible that Boulton felt that while he had spent £2,000 in promoting Argand's lamp, it would be throwing good money after bad to make a further investment, and therefore employed the simple stratagem of ignoring the shoals of letters from Argand which entreated him to come to London or to Paris and do something about the patent.

On 31 July 1784, while supervising his Cornish tin mines, Boulton found time to write a very despondent letter to Argand, ostensibly instructing him in improvements he could make to his lamp, but continuing in the mournful vein: 'I have been very low spirited ever since I have been here, the springs of life seem to be let down, and I have no powers or inclination for business. I live here in a lonely house about a mile from the mines, I have no neighbour, friend or companion, but have lately sent for my son.' Boulton had the grace, however, to end with the following: 'I may have my doubts, jealousies and fears of ninety-nine per cent of mankind, but I assure you that they do not extend to you, being persuaded that you are a man of ten thousand, and that I am happy in subscribing myself, dear sir, your affectionate friend, Matthew Boulton.'

Regrettably, one must assume that this picture of the 'lonely house' was a distortion

FRAˢ. PIEᵉ. AMI ARGAND~MARCET, NÉ A GENEVE

Inventeur des ~ Lampes à Courant d'Air

of the truth to suit his own ends. James Watt once described Cosgarne, Boulton's house near Truro, as a 'most delightful place, a neat roomy house with sash-windows, double breadth, the wall to the south covered with vines loaded with young grapes, a walled garden with excellent peaches and plums, plenty of currants, two orchards and a lawn before the door'!

Argand had first written to Boulton in May 1784, stating that a French acquaintance had tried to persuade him to go to Paris to patent the lamp, but that he would rather place his trust in Boulton. He had made several improvements and hoped for better fortune. The most essential part of the lamp was the form of the wick and the use of a tall glass chimney through which air was drawn. Primarily, the lamp had twin branches, and the pressure of the air combined with the oil which ignited it. Argand recommended spermatic or whale oil, but when the lamp was lit in the Science Museum a century later olive oil burned very well.

In Argand's own words: 'What shows plainly that the glass chimnies must be made on purpose, narrow enough to become hot, and heat the current of air very much, is the necessity of flattening the glasses for the straight flat wicks and making them oval, for if they are left round, then they make little or no heat.' Argand applied himself seriously to his task, requesting the services of Mr Ramsden, a distinguished tool or instrument maker and a skilled glass-blower, who had supplied both Captain Cook and Sir Joseph Banks with navigational instruments.

There followed a series of letters from Argand to Boulton, the most interesting of which consisted of a mention by Josiah Wedgwood that when the latter visited Soho, he would stop to see 'the business of the lamps'. This was in order, presumably, to examine how they could be applied to Wedgwood vases. It is interesting that Argand's letters to Boulton were written in immaculate English, with far better punctuation than any of Boulton's British correspondents, although Argand stated (probably in relation to a trial which Boulton would have to attend regarding the newly-proposed coinage) that he 'would support Boulton in his broken English'.

Finally, having written letter after letter to Boulton with no response, Argand lost patience: 'Dear Sir, Your absence proves fatal to me, unhappy that I am, I lose my fortune by it.' In the course of a very long letter, Argand stated that although he had been implored by his French friends in high places to come to Paris to work on his lamp there, the opportunity had by then been lost. He continued: '. . . although the lamp is now in a state of perfection, as for the burner and means of supplying oil, I don't see at all how we would get for the next winter a sufficient number of lamps to supply both London and Paris. Had we 2 or 300 hands at work, we would still fall short of the sale – but everything, every circumstance, has turned against me.

'Relying on the Soho Manufactory, I never thought it proper to put any more men to work in town than those Mr Parker got at Penton's [a metalworking firm] who have themselves worked very little. During the time of my illness [he suffered greatly from rheumatism] I was prevented from being daily about them.' Mr Parker, having introduced Argand to Boulton, was as inefficient as the workmen as it turned out: he added to his failures by accepting far more orders for lamps than could possibly be supplied, and this placed even greater pressures on Argand.

Argand proceeded to berate himself for his gullibility, stating that everyone who knew him thought he was making a fortune, and yet he was on the brink of ruin. He was fearful that he had lost the patronage of the Viscomte De St Priest: 'He will abandon me and forsake me forever, and I shall irrevocably lose my best friend and patron, who has done for me more than a father, and whose esteem and friendship is the more precious advantage I can enjoy in France, and through whose favour and power everything may be obtained there.'

The remainder of Argand's correspondence with Boulton was very bitter. But almost at the end of their association, in 1786, he had the generosity to write: 'Having every reason to consider my patent as lost inexorably, I now employ my time into getting into some arrangement with Messrs March, Parker and Howard. They are all of them very willing to alleviate my misfortune, and I cannot help thinking that it is owing in a great measure of generous dispositions towards me that they have seen in you, and on that account, as well as on every occasion that has brought us together, you are, and shall be blessed by me.'

The above-mentioned gentlemen devised a plan whereby a City ironmonger or 'tin-man' named William Slark, of Cheapside, should sell the lamps, with the proceeds to be divided between the partners. This undertaking was presumably successful, as Argand's debts were considerably reduced.

Still hopeful of even greater success, Argand set up a factory in his home town, Versoix, near Geneva, into which he poured the remainder of his fortune of about

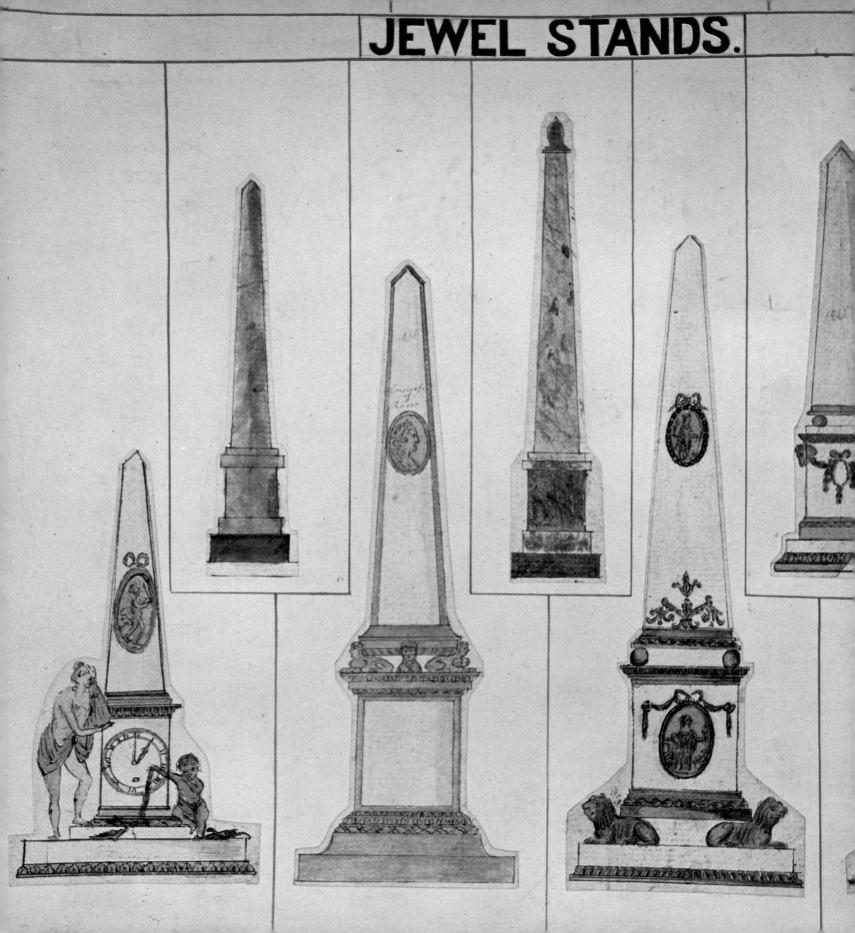

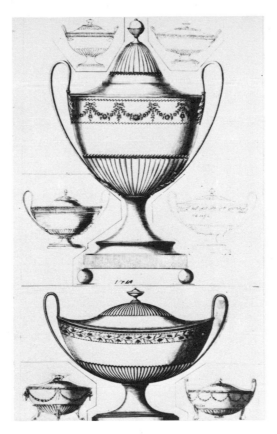

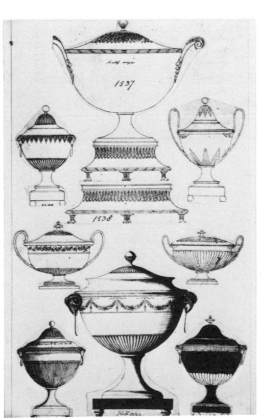

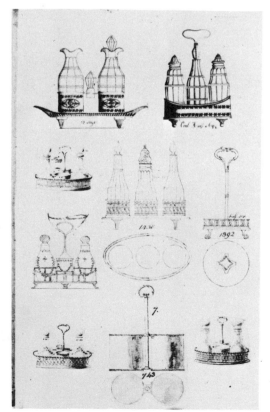

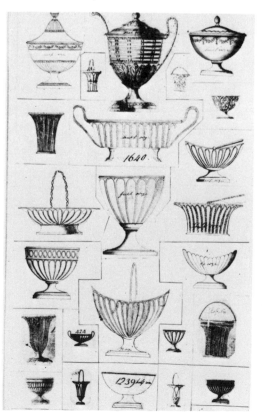

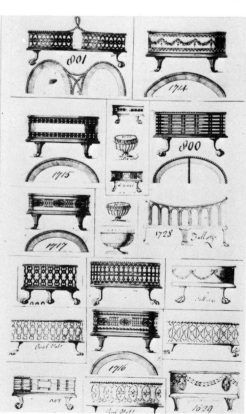

THE MYND FAMILY

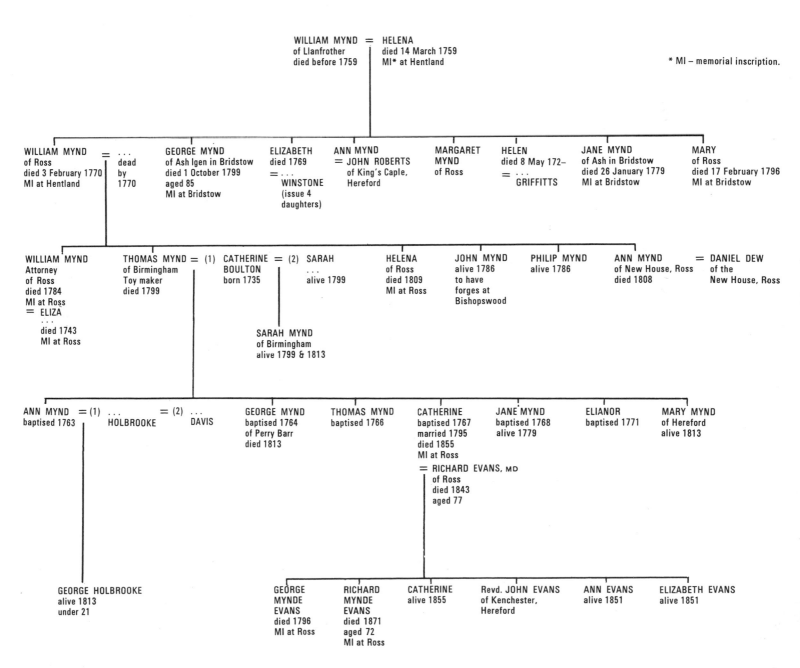

WILLIAM MYND = HELENA
of Llanfrother   died 14 March 1759
died before 1759   MI* at Hentland

* MI – memorial inscription.

WILLIAM MYND = ...   GEORGE MYND   ELIZABETH   ANN MYND   MARGARET   HELEN   JANE MYND   MARY
of Ross   dead   of Ash Igen in Bridstow died 1769   = JOHN ROBERTS   MYND   died 8 May 172–   of Ash in Bridstow   of Ross
died 3 February 1770 by   died 1 October 1799   = ...   of King's Caple,   of Ross   = . . .   died 26 January 1779   died 17 February 1796
MI at Hentland 1770   aged 85   WINSTONE   Hereford   GRIFFITTS   MI at Bridstow   MI at Bridstow
                          MI at Bridstow   (issue 4
                                                   daughters)

WILLIAM MYND   THOMAS MYND = (1) CATHERINE = (2) SARAH   HELENA   JOHN MYND   PHILIP MYND   ANN MYND   = DANIEL DEW
Attorney   of Birmingham   BOULTON   . . .   of Ross   alive 1786   alive 1786   of New House, Ross   of the
of Ross   Toy maker   born 1735   alive 1799   died 1809   to have   died 1808   New House, Ross
died 1784   died 1799   MI at Ross   forges at
MI at Ross   Bishopswood
= ELIZA   SARAH MYND
  . . .   of Birmingham
  died 1743   alive 1799 & 1813
  MI at Ross

ANN MYND = (1) . . .   = (2) . . .   GEORGE MYND   THOMAS MYND   CATHERINE   JANE MYND   ELIANOR   MARY MYND
baptised 1763   HOLBROOKE   DAVIS   baptised 1764   baptised 1766   baptised 1767   baptised 1768   baptised 1771   of Hereford
                                         of Perry Barr   married 1795   alive 1779   alive 1813
                                         died 1813   died 1855
                                                                            MI at Ross
                                                                            = RICHARD EVANS, MD
                                                                              of Ross
                                                                              died 1843
                                                                              aged 77

GEORGE HOLBROOKE   GEORGE   RICHARD   CATHERINE   Revd. JOHN EVANS   ANN EVANS   ELIZABETH EVANS
alive 1813   MYNDE   MYNDE   alive 1855   of Kenchester,   alive 1851   alive 1851
under 21   EVANS   EVANS   Hereford
                                         died 1796   died 1871
                                         MI at Ross   aged 72
                                                      MI at Ross

135